Billy Swift
Goes to Space School

and

Bears
on the
Brain

Written by
Robin Twiddy

Illustrated by
Emre Karacan

4

Billy Swift
Goes to Space School

Written by
Robin Twiddy

Illustrated by
Emre Karacan

Chapter One

Better than the Bus

There was nothing special about Billy. He had always been just a normal kid, until recently. Billy was starting at Space School, and he would be the first human to ever go there. This made him very special indeed.

Billy had always loved space. His room was full of books on space, toy spaceships, and posters of the stars. His favourite video game was Intergalactic Space Bounce. It was a little like football but with rocket ships and lasers. Billy was very good at Intergalactic Space Bounce. In fact, Billy was so good at the game that he had the highest score in the world.

There was a loud, thundering sound from outside. Billy ran to the window in time to see the large spaceship land in the street outside his house. Today was going to be the best day ever! Billy grabbed his bag and leapt down the stairs. He was so excited to start his first day at Space School.

Billy ran up the ramp and found a seat on the spaceship. Even the seats were better than the ones on his old school bus.

Billy looked around him and saw that the spaceship must have been to some other planets on the way to Earth because there were some strange-looking kids already in the other seats.

There were Zargons from Zargonia, with their purple skin and three-elbowed arms. There were Truples from Trupter Five – they only had one eye on a stalk that came out of the top of their heads. There were kids from all the planets that made up the Intergalactic Partnership. But Billy was the only human.

Chapter Two

Welcome to Space School

The spaceship sped through the sky and out of Earth's atmosphere in seconds. Even though Space School was the other side of the galaxy, the spaceship made it there in minutes.

"I guess I won't be doing my homework on the bus anymore," Billy said excitedly to the girl next to him.

Billy looked out of the window as the spaceship slowed down to dock at Space School. The school itself was a large space station that orbited a big, purple planet. It was the best thing Billy had ever seen. He checked his tablet computer, which had his classes and a map of the school on it, to see where he needed to go.

As soon as Billy had stepped off the spaceship, he was greeted by Mr Gargon. Mr Gargon was from a water planet called Aquatar. He looked like a sea monster, but a kind sea monster. He had fins and gills and big, dark, wet eyes.

"Welcome, Billy. We are very pleased to have our first human student at Space School," Mr Gargon said. "Now don't worry if you get some funny looks from the other children," Mr Gargon went on. "Most of them have never seen a human before."

"Billy," Mr Gargon said. "If you step into the transport tube and tell it where you need to be, it will take you straight there."
Billy stepped into the tube and said, "Room 4B". Then... WHOOSH! He flew up into the air. The next thing Billy knew, he was stood at the front of a class full of students.

Chapter Three

The Classroom

"Class, I would like you to give a warm Space School welcome to our newest student, Billy Swift," said green orb at the front of the class. "I am Mrs Hurl," she added.

"Hello, Billy," said the students together.

"Please take a seat over there next to Norbin," Mrs Hurl said.

Billy took the empty seat next to what must
have been Norbin, a short and dumpy boy
who appeared to be made of rocks. Even his
glasses seemed to be made of rocks. When
Billy sat down, something wet and sticky hit
him in the back of his head.

The whole class laughed as Billy wiped black ink from the back of his head. At the back of the class was a kid with tentacles for arms. He looked like a squid that had been stuffed into trousers and a shirt. One of his tentacles was dripping with ink.

"That's Trent Tentacular," said Norbin. "He is the captain of the hyper ball team."

Chapter Four

In Space, No One Cares

Billy wasn't feeling quite as excited about his first day at Space School anymore. It turned out that being the new kid, even in space, was hard. The first class of the day was Zero-G Maths. It was just like maths on Earth but without any gravity.

Solving maths problems whilst floating around was hard. Billy tried to enjoy it, but Trent kept making fun of him.

Later on, in Alien Languages 101, Trent made fun of the way he said things, even though he had never spoken Zargonian before.

After that, they had Intergalactic History. They learnt about a race called the Toxlings who had tried to turn every planet into a toxic waste dump. Trent said that Earth already was a toxic waste dump. All the other children laughed.

TOXLING

The last class of the day was PE. After all the other classes, Billy wasn't looking forward to Trent making a fool out of him again. They would be playing hyper ball, and Trent was the captain of the team. Even worse, Billy was on the other team.

Chapter Five

The Big Game

When the teams were picked, Billy was handed a control pad.

"What's this?" he asked.

"You use that to control your drone," said Norbin.

A large screen appeared on the wall in front of the class. It showed a group of rocket ships and a giant energy ball.

"They must be in space outside the station," thought Billy.

The game was simple. At either end of the play-zone was a goal. Each team had to knock the energy ball with their lasers into the other team's goal.

"This is just like Intergalactic Space Bounce," thought Billy.

Trent looked over at Billy and laughed.

"You are going down, Earthling," Trent said with confidence.

Billy smiled to himself. He held the highest score on Earth for Intergalactic Space Bounce.

It didn't take long for Billy to get the hang of the game. Within five minutes, he had mastered the controls. Soon, Trent realised what was happening. Even though he had picked all the best players for his side, they were losing. Billy's ship was zooming all over the place, dodging lasers and scoring goals.

After ten minutes, the game was over, and Billy's team had won. At the end of the game, the whole class surprised Billy, picking him up and bouncing him in the air, chanting his name. Even Trent came over and held out his tentacle.

"You were really good out there. We could use you on the team," he said.

Maybe Space School wasn't going to be so bad after all.

Billy Swift Goes to Space School

1. Can you describe what the Zargons looked like?

2. What hit Billy in the back of the head?

3. Which language had Billy never spoken before?

    (a) Zargonian

    (b) Aquatarian

    (c) Trupterian

4. What was the third class of the day?

5. Why do you think Trent made fun of Billy? What
    would you have done if you were Billy?

Bears
on the
Brain

Written by
Robin Twiddy

Illustrated by
Emre Karacan

It was the summer holidays and Phil was having a great time. He had played with his friends, flown kites and even taken a trip to a theme park, but soon the holidays would be over. The park in his town had just had a new playground built and it looked brilliant, and he really wanted to visit it!

There was a zip line, climbing frames, spinning seats, seesaws, huge swings and giant slides. There was even a cart in the middle of the playground that sold ice cream. Phil had been excited about the new playground for the whole summer holidays.

Today was the day. His mum had promised that they would go to the grand opening of the playground and spend all afternoon there. She said that he could eat as much ice cream as he liked. Phil couldn't wait. There was only one problem. Mum said she had to do lots of chores around town before they could go to the park, and Phil had to come too.

Whilst Mum got together all the things they would need for a morning in town and then an afternoon at the park, Phil read his favourite book, 'Bears and What They Do in the Woods'. Phil loved this book, and he must have read it a thousand times. He didn't know why he liked bears so much, but he just did.

"Phil, are you ready?" called Phil's mum.

Phil ran down the stairs with the book in his hand.

"Did you know that brown bears sleep for around two hundred days?" Phil said. "That's called hibernation."

"You have bears on the brain! Put that book down and get your shoes on," said Mum.

When Phil and his mum got to the bus stop, there was a large, hairy man sat on the bench. He was waiting for the bus, too. His thick beard reminded Phil of the shaggy fur of brown bears, but he didn't think any more of it. The bus had arrived.

BEARS
WHAT
THEY do in
THE WOODS

Phil climbed up the step onto the bus and his mum got her purse out to pay. When she handed the money over to the bus driver, Phil noticed the bus driver's hands were a bit strange. They were very big, and the backs had more hair on them than he had ever seen on a hand.

Phil's mum sat him down before he could get a good look at the driver. He asked his mum if she had noticed anything strange or bear-like about the driver.

"Phil, you have bears on the brain! Some people just have hairy hands," she answered.

Once they were in town, his mum took him
to the fishmonger. Right there, behind the
counter, was a bear. It was wearing a striped
red-and-white apron and was cutting up fish.
There was no denying it – a bear was working
in the fishmongers! It was as plain as the nose
on his face.

"M-M-Mum, did you see th-th-that bear behind the counter?" Phil stammered. He couldn't believe his eyes. This wasn't a man who looked a bit like a bear... This was a bear! A polar bear to be exact.

"Phil, I have already told you. There are no bears in our country except for in zoos," his mum said as they walked away.

Phil knew what he had seen. He had seen a bear. He had seen a bear doing human things! Next, they needed to go to the post office. When they got to the post office there was a long queue stretching back from the counter. Phil and his mum joined the back of it. Phil looked along the queue. There was a man with a stack of boxes, a woman with an envelope, and in front of her, was a very hairy man in a dark suit.

"Look, Mum, another bear. Can you see his fur?"

"That is just Mr Johnson. He works at the bank," his mum said. "You have bears on the brain again! Am I going to have to take that book away from you?"

When it was his mum's turn at the counter, Phil got a good look at the postwoman who was handing his mum her parcel. There was no mistaking it. She was a bear. "How many bears work at the post office?" he wondered. Was the postman who delivered mail to his house a bear too?

The bear at the counter handed Phil a lollipop and smiled at him. She had scary, pointed teeth, but her smile was kind. He took the lollipop with a shaking hand.
"Th-thank you," he stammered. Looking the bear in the eye, he knew she was an Asian black bear.

As they were leaving the post office, Phil looked at his mum. He was going to ask her if she had seen the bear too, but he changed his mind when he saw the look on her face. He knew exactly what she would say...
"Phil, you have bears on the brain!"

When they were outside in the street, his mum asked if Phil was ready to go to the playground now. Phil had been waiting for this all summer, but now all he could think about was bears.

"Bears, bears everywhere, and even on the brain," he thought.

On the way to the park, Phil saw more and more bears, but his mum didn't seem to notice at all. There were black bears, there were brown bears, there were panda bears and there were grizzly bears, and all of them were wearing people's clothes and going about doing people things.

Finally, Phil was at the park. All the waiting had been worth it. But as he looked out across the playground, all he could see was bears. Bears on the zipline, bears on the seesaw, bears on the swings... Even the ice cream man was a bear!

Phil turned to his mum. He was going to say, "Look, can't you see them? They are all bears! Everyone is a bear!" but the words stuck in his mouth. Looking down at him was a bear in his mum's clothes.

"What's the matter, Phil? You don't have bears on the brain again, do you?" said Mum.

Then Phil looked down at where his hands
should have been, but he didn't have hands
anymore. No, he had brown, furry paws!
"This is ridiculous," Phil thought. "Talk about
bears on the brain!"
And at that moment, he woke up...

"Phil, did you have a good hibernation?" his bear-mother asked, as he climbed out of his bear-bed. "I let you sleep for a few extra days because you looked so comfy."

"I had the strangest dream," said Phil. "I was a human and so were you!"

"Well, maybe you shouldn't be reading things like this before you hibernate," Mum said, holding up his copy of 'Humans and What They Do in the Town'.

"I guess I had people on the brain," Phil said, smiling, as he took the book in his paw.

Bears on the Brain

1. What did the cart in the middle of the playground sell?

2. Can you describe the people that were in the queue at the post office?

3. What did the bear at the counter hand Phil?
   (a) A chocolate
   (b) A lollipop
   (c) A sticker

4. What kind of bears did Phil see on the way to the park?

5. How do you think Phil felt when his mum wouldn't believe him? Have you ever felt like this?

©This edition published 2021.
First published in 2020.
BookLife Publishing Ltd.
King's Lynn, Norfolk PE30 4LS

ISBN 978-1-83927-025-3

Billy Swift Goes to Space School and Bears on the Brain
Written by Robin Twiddy
Illustrated by Emre Karacan

An Introduction to BookLife Readers...

Our Readers have been specifically created in line with the London Institute of Education's approach to book banding and are phonetically decodable and ordered to support each phase of the Letters and Sounds document.

Each book has been created to provide the best possible reading and learning experience. Our aim is to share our love of books with children, providing both emerging readers and prolific page-turners with beautiful books that are guaranteed to provoke interest and learning, regardless of ability.

BOOK BAND GRADED using the Institute of Education's approach to levelling.

PHONETICALLY DECODABLE supporting each phase of Letters and Sounds.

EXERCISES AND QUESTIONS to offer reinforcement and to ascertain comprehension.

BEAUTIFULLY ILLUSTRATED to inspire and provoke engagement, providing a variety of styles for the reader to enjoy whilst reading through the series.

AUTHOR INSIGHT:
ROBIN TWIDDY

Robin Twiddy is one of BookLife Publishing's most creative and prolific editorial talents, who imbues all his copy with a sense of adventure and energy. Robin's Cambridge-based first class honours degree in psychosocial studies offers a unique viewpoint on factual information and allows him to relay information in a manner that readers of any age are guaranteed to retain. He also holds a certificate in Teaching in the Lifelong Sector, and a postgraduate certificate in Consumer Psychology.

A father of two, Robin has written over 70 titles for BookLife and specialises in conceptual, role-playing narratives which promote interaction with the reader and inspire even the most reluctant of readers to fully engage with his books.

This book focuses on developing independence, fluency and comprehension. It is a lime level 11 book band.